· BRUNCH ·

the perfect weekend treat

· BRUNCH ·

the perfect weekend treat

Jennifer Donovan

p

This is a Parragon Publishing Book
This edition published in 2006

Parragon Publishing
Queen Street House
4 Queen Street
Bath BA1 1HE
United Kingdom

Produced by
The Bridgewater Book Company
Lewes, East Sussex BN7 2NZ
United Kingdom

Photographer Calvey Taylor-Haw
Home Economist Ruth Pollock

ISBN 1-40543-703-0
Printed in China

Notes for the reader

- This book uses imperial, metric, or US cup measurements. Follow the same units of measurement throughout; do not mix imperial and metric.
- All spoon measurements are level: teaspoons are assumed to be 5 ml, and tablespoons are assumed to be 15 ml.
- Unless otherwise stated, milk is assumed to be whole, eggs, and individual vegetables such as carrots are medium, and pepper is freshly ground black pepper.
- Recipes using raw eggs should be avoided by infants, the elderly, pregnant women, convalescents, and anyone suffering from an illness.

contents

introduction

Brunch is my favorite meal of the week. After a wonderfully long Sunday lie-in, without the distraction of alarm clocks and the pressures of work, there is truly nothing better than a delicious midmorning feast that somehow drifts over into lunch.

Taking time out from a busy life is vital, and brunch provides the perfect opportunity. Curl up and indulge with freshly baked muffins and just a newspaper for company. Invite a group of friends around to share this casual meal with you, allowing the morning to meander gently into the afternoon, knowing that the world can wait.

Brunch has no rules. Mellow and relaxed or upbeat and lively, brunch food can always fit the mood. From fresh pastries or traditional bacon and eggs to spicy chorizo tortilla, just about anything goes.

Filled with recipes ranging from the traditional to the more innovative, this book is designed to inspire. No matter what your level of culinary skill, you will find that every chapter is packed with a selection of fabulous recipes that can be adapted to feed from two people to ten, with stunning results for you and your family and friends to enjoy.

Brunch is my favorite meal of the week

sweet

sweet moments

It is no accident that the first chapter of this book is devoted to all things sweet. After all, who can possibly resist the smell of warm muffins or pastries mingled with the aroma of freshly brewed coffee? I have included my two favorite muffin recipes—the dried cherries in the Dried Cherry Cheesecake Muffins provide a slight tang to balance out the sweetness, while the cinnamon sugar-topped Doughnut Muffins will satisfy the sweetest tooth.

For more adventurous cooks, a traditional recipe for croissants is included. Although croissants are now available from just about every bakery, nothing tastes better than the homemade version made with fresh butter. At first the recipe may look daunting, but most of the time involved is in leaving the yeast to do its work. Shorten the process by starting the croissant dough the night before you need it and leaving it to rise slowly in the refrigerator while you sleep.

For a slightly healthier start to the day, the Citrus Fruit and Ginger Compote with an infusion of lemon grass, cardamom, and honey, is irresistible. Granola makes an excellent brunch appetizer crumbled over a bowl of plain yogurt and is surprisingly quick and easy to make. Both recipes can be made well in advance so that you can catch a few extra hours' sleep.

French Toast has long been a favorite, but making large batches in the traditional method with a skillet is time-consuming. The version given here makes preparing French Toast for six as easy as it is for one.

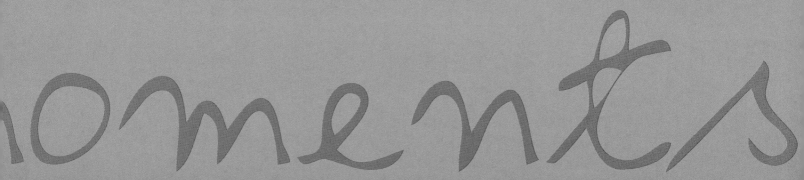

The dried cherries are mixed in with the flour to prevent them from sinking to the bottom of the muffins and to ensure that they are evenly distributed. Try the same technique with your favorite fruitcake recipe! Dried cranberries also work well here.

Dried Cherry Cheesecake Muffins

MAKES 12 MUFFINS

Preheat the oven to 350°F/180°C. Grease a deep 12-cup muffin pan.

Melt the butter and let cool slightly. In a large bowl, whisk the cream cheese and sugar together, add the eggs one at a time until well combined, and then stir in the melted butter.

Mix the flour and cherries together in a bowl, then stir gently into the batter. Spoon into the prepared muffin pan, filling each hole to about two-thirds full, and bake for 12–15 minutes, or until golden brown. Remove from the oven and let cool on a wire rack. Eat warm or cold, dusted lightly with confectioners' sugar.

INGREDIENTS

5½ oz/150 g butter, plus extra
  for greasing
scant 1 cup cream cheese
generous ¾ cup superfine sugar
3 large eggs, lightly beaten
2 cups self-rising flour
generous ½ cup dried cherries, chopped
confectioners' sugar, for dusting

It is important to brush the warm muffins with melted butter and sprinkle the cinnamon and sugar mixture over them immediately. If you wait too long, the butter will sink into the muffins and the sugar will not stick.

Doughnut Muffins

INGREDIENTS
6 oz/175 g butter, softened, plus extra
    for greasing
1 cup superfine sugar
2 large eggs, lightly beaten
generous 2½ cups all-purpose flour
¾ tbsp baking powder
¼ tsp baking soda
pinch of salt
½ tsp freshly grated nutmeg
generous 1 cup milk
TOPPING
½ cup superfine sugar
1 tsp ground cinnamon
2 tbsp butter, melted

MAKES 12 MUFFINS
Preheat the oven to 350°F/180°C. Grease a deep 12-cup muffin pan.

In a large bowl, beat the butter and sugar together until light and creamy. Add the eggs, a little at a time, beating well between additions.

Sift the flour, baking powder, baking soda, salt, and nutmeg together. Add half to the creamed mixture with half of the milk. Gently fold the ingredients together before incorporating the remaining flour and milk. Spoon the mixture into the prepared muffin pan, filling each hole to about two-thirds full. Bake for 15–20 minutes, or until the muffins are lightly brown and firm to the touch.

For the topping, mix the sugar and cinnamon together. While the muffins are still warm from the oven, brush lightly with melted butter, and sprinkle over the cinnamon and sugar mixture. Eat warm or cold.

Start this recipe the night before. Make the dough and roll out the croissants, then brush with the glaze, cover with plastic wrap and refrigerate overnight. The next morning, let prove for 30–45 minutes, then proceed as per the recipe.

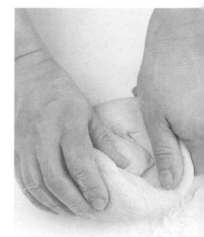

Fresh Croissants

MAKES 12 CROISSANTS

Preheat the oven to 400°F/200°C. Stir the dry ingredients into a large bowl, make a well in the center, and add the milk. Mix to a soft dough, adding more milk if too dry. Knead on a lightly floured counter for 5–10 minutes, or until smooth and elastic. Let rise in a large greased bowl, covered, in a warm place until doubled in size. Meanwhile, flatten the butter with a rolling pin between 2 sheets of waxed paper to form a rectangle about ¼ inch/5 mm thick, then let chill.

Knead the dough for 1 minute. Remove the butter from the refrigerator and let soften slightly. Roll out the dough on a well floured counter to 18 x 6 inches/ 46 x 15 cm. Place the butter in the center, folding up the sides and squeezing the edges together gently. With the short end of the dough toward you, fold the top third down toward the center, then fold the bottom third up. Rotate 90° clockwise so that the fold is to your left and the top flap toward your right. Roll out to a rectangle and fold again. If the butter feels soft, wrap the dough in plastic wrap, and let chill. Repeat the rolling process twice more. Cut the dough in half. Roll out one half into a triangle ¼ inch/5 mm thick (keep the other half refrigerated). Use a cardboard triangular template, base 7 inches/ 18 cm and sides 8 inches/20 cm, to cut out the croissants.

Brush the triangles lightly with the glaze. Roll into croissant shapes, starting at the base and tucking the point underneath to prevent unrolling while cooking. Brush again with the glaze. Place on an ungreased baking sheet and let double in size. Bake for 15–20 minutes until golden brown.

INGREDIENTS

1 lb 2 oz/500 g white bread flour, plus extra for rolling

scant ¼ cup superfine sugar

1 tsp salt

2 tsp active dry yeast

1¼ cups milk, heated until just warm to the touch

10½ oz/300 g butter, softened, plus extra for greasing

1 egg, lightly beaten with 1 tbsp milk, for glazing

The Banana Bread can be stored in the freezer for up to three months. Thaw overnight in the refrigerator before serving. The bread can also be frosted for a delicious teatime treat.

Banana Bread with Strawberry Compote & Mascarpone

INGREDIENTS

4½ oz/125 g butter, softened, plus extra
    for greasing
½ cup superfine sugar
generous ¼ cup brown sugar
3 eggs
1 tsp vanilla extract
3 large ripe bananas
scant 2 cups self-rising flour
1 tsp freshly grated nutmeg
1 tsp ground cinnamon
STRAWBERRY COMPOTE
scant ½ cup brown sugar
juice of 2 oranges
grated rind of 1 orange
1 cinnamon stick
2½ cups strawberries, thickly sliced
confectioners' sugar, sifted, for dusting
mascarpone or plain yogurt, to serve

SERVES 8

Preheat the oven to 350°F/180°C. Grease a 9 x 4¼-inch/23 x 11-cm loaf pan and line the bottom with parchment paper.

Place the butter and sugars in a bowl and beat together until light and fluffy. Add the eggs, one at a time, then mix in the vanilla extract. Peel the bananas and mash coarsely with the back of a fork. Stir gently into the butter mixture, then add the flour, nutmeg, and cinnamon, stirring until just combined.

Pour the mixture into the prepared pan and bake for 1 hour 15 minutes, or until a skewer inserted into the center comes out clean. Remove from the oven and let stand for 5 minutes before turning out onto a wire rack.

To make the compote, mix the brown sugar, orange juice, orange rind, and cinnamon stick together in a medium pan and bring to a boil. Add the strawberries and return to a boil. Remove from the heat, pour into a clean heatproof bowl, and let cool. Serve slices of the banana bread with a dollop of mascarpone or yogurt and spoon over the warm or cold compote. Dust with sifted confectioners' sugar.

As the batter sits, it tends to thicken up and can make the pancakes very doughy. If the mixture becomes too thick while you are cooking the pancakes, add a little extra milk before continuing.

Apple Pancakes with Maple Syrup Butter

MAKES 18 PANCAKES TO SERVE 4–6

Mix the flour, sugar, and cinnamon together in a bowl and make a well in the center. Beat the egg and the milk together and pour into the well. Using a wooden spoon, gently incorporate the dry ingredients into the liquid until well combined, then stir in the grated apple.

Heat the butter in a large nonstick skillet over low heat until melted and bubbling. Add tablespoons of the pancake mixture to form 3½-inch/9-cm circles. Cook each pancake for about 1 minute, until it starts to bubble lightly on the top and looks set, then flip it over and cook the other side for 30 seconds, or until cooked through. The pancakes should be golden brown; if not, increase the heat a little. Remove from the skillet and keep warm. Repeat the process until all of the pancake batter has been used up (it is not necessary to add extra butter).

To make the maple syrup butter, melt the butter with the maple syrup in a pan over low heat and stir until combined. To serve, place the pancakes on serving dishes and spoon over the flavored butter. Serve warm.

INGREDIENTS
scant 1½ cups self-rising flour
½ cup superfine sugar
1 tsp ground cinnamon
1 egg
scant 1 cup milk
2 apples, peeled and grated
1 tsp butter
MAPLE SYRUP BUTTER
3 oz/85 g butter, softened
3 tbsp maple syrup

To vary the flavor, try different dried fruits such as apricots, raisins, or prunes as well as dried seeds and nuts. As the granola cools, break up any large pieces that have formed with your hands.

Homemade Granola

INGREDIENTS
generous 2¾ cups rolled oats

2 Granny Smith or similar tart apples, peeled and diced

scant ⅔ cup dried figs, chopped

½ cup slivered almonds

2 tbsp honey

¼ cup cold water

1 tsp ground cinnamon

1 tsp vanilla extract

1 tsp butter, melted, for greasing

plain yogurt, to serve

SERVES 6–8
Preheat the oven to 325°F/160°C. Mix the oats, apples, figs, and almonds together in a large bowl. Bring the honey, water, cinnamon, and vanilla extract to a boil in a pan, then pour over the oat mixture, stirring well to make sure that all the ingredients are coated.

Lightly grease a large baking sheet with the butter and spread the oat mixture out evenly on the sheet. Bake for 40–45 minutes, or until the granola is golden brown, stirring with a fork from time to time to break up any lumps. Pour onto a clean baking sheet and let cool before storing in an airtight container. Serve sprinkled over bowls of fresh plain yogurt.

Use firm but ripe bananas for this recipe, as softer bananas may disintegrate too easily. Try pears or strawberries for a delicious change.

Waffles with Caramelized Bananas

MAKES 12 WAFFLES TO SERVE 4–6

Mix the flour, baking powder, salt, and sugar together in a bowl. Whisk the egg yolks, milk, and melted butter together with a fork, then stir this mixture into the dry ingredients to make a smooth batter.

Using an electric mixer or hand whisk, whisk the egg whites in a clean glass bowl until stiff peaks form. Fold into the batter mixture. Spoon 2 large tablespoons of the batter into a preheated waffle maker and cook according to the manufacturer's instructions.

To make the caramelized bananas, melt the butter with the corn syrup in a pan over low heat and stir until combined. Let simmer for a few minutes until the caramel thickens and darkens slightly. Add the bananas and mix gently to coat. Pour over the warm waffles and serve at once.

INGREDIENTS
scant 1¼ cups all-purpose flour
2 tsp baking powder
½ tsp salt
2 tsp superfine sugar
2 eggs, separated
generous 1 cup milk
3 oz/85 g butter, melted
CARAMELIZED BANANAS
3½ oz/100 g butter, cut into pieces
3 tbsp corn syrup
3 large ripe bananas, peeled and
   thickly sliced

This oven-baked method of French Toast uses much less fat than the pan-fried version and makes it easy to produce larger quantities.

Spiced French Toast with Seasonal Berries

INGREDIENTS
4 eggs, plus 1 extra egg white
¼ tsp ground cinnamon
¼ tsp allspice
4 slices thick white bread
1 tbsp butter, melted
BERRIES
scant ½ cup superfine sugar
¼ cup freshly squeezed
   orange juice
scant 2 cups mixed seasonal berries,
   such as strawberries, raspberries,
   and blueberries

SERVES 4
Preheat the oven to 425°F/220°C. Place the eggs and egg white in a large shallow bowl and whisk together with a fork. Add the cinnamon and allspice and whisk until combined.

Soak the bread slices in the egg mixture for about 1 minute on each side. Brush a large baking sheet with the melted butter and place the bread slices on the sheet. Bake for 5–7 minutes, or until lightly browned. Turn the slices over and continue to bake for an additional 2–3 minutes.

Meanwhile, place the sugar and orange juice in a medium pan and bring to a boil over low heat, stirring to dissolve the sugar. Add the berries, turn off the heat, and let cool for 10 minutes. Serve spooned over the toast.

These cinnamon rolls are best eaten warm, on the same day they are made. As a variation, add 2 tablespoons of raisins to the filling and proceed as per the recipe.

Simple Cinnamon Rolls

MAKES 8 ROLLS

Preheat the oven to 350°F/180°C. Grease an 8-inch/20-cm round pan and line the bottom with parchment paper.

Mix the flour, salt, superfine sugar, and cinnamon together in a bowl. Whisk the butter, egg yolks, and milk together and combine with the dry ingredients to make a soft dough. Turn out onto a large piece of waxed paper, lightly sprinkled with flour, and roll out to a rectangle 12 x 10 inches/30 x 25 cm.

To make the filling, mix the ingredients together, spread evenly over the dough and roll up, jelly-roll style, to form a log. Using a sharp knife, cut the dough into 8 even-size slices and pack into the prepared pan. Brush gently with extra milk and bake for 30–35 minutes, or until golden brown. Remove from the oven and let cool for 5 minutes before removing from the pan.

Sift the confectioners' sugar into a large bowl and make a well in the center. Place the cream cheese and butter in the center, pour over the water, and stir to mix. Add extra boiling water, a few drops at a time, until the frosting coats the back of a spoon. Stir in the vanilla extract. Drizzle over the rolls. Serve warm or cold.

INGREDIENTS

scant 2½ cups self-rising flour

pinch of salt

2 tbsp superfine sugar

1 tsp ground cinnamon

3½ oz/100 g butter, melted, plus extra for greasing

2 egg yolks

scant 1 cup milk, plus extra for glazing

FILLING

1 tsp ground cinnamon

generous ¼ cup brown sugar

2 tbsp superfine sugar

1 tbsp butter, melted

FROSTING

generous 1 cup confectioners' sugar, sifted

2 tbsp cream cheese, softened

1 tbsp butter, softened

about 2 tbsp boiling water

1 tsp vanilla extract

Lemon grass is widely available in large supermarkets. If you have trouble finding it, substitute some very finely grated lemon rind instead.

Citrus Fruit & Ginger Compote

INGREDIENTS

4 oranges

1 lemon grass stalk

⅔ cup freshly squeezed
  orange juice

½-inch/1-cm piece fresh gingerroot,
  peeled and sliced

4 cardamom pods, lightly crushed

4 cloves

2 tbsp honey

TO SERVE

4 tbsp plain yogurt

1 tbsp slivered almonds, toasted

SERVES 4

Peel the oranges, cut into thick slices, and place in a bowl. Trim the lemon grass to retain the bottom third or white part of the stalk. Peel away the outer layers, retaining the tender center, and dice finely.

Combine the orange juice, ginger, cardamom pods, cloves, diced lemon grass, and honey in a pan and bring to a boil. Let simmer for 1 minute, then let cool.

When cool, strain the mixture over the sliced oranges, cover, and let chill in the refrigerator for 1 hour or overnight. Serve in individual dishes with a spoonful of yogurt and a sprinkling of toasted slivered almonds.

the pen

get cracking—
the perfect egg

Brunch wouldn't be brunch without eggs. They are possibly the most versatile of all foods, and this chapter covers myriad exciting ways in which they can be used.

One of the most popular choices for brunch has always been Eggs Benedict, but so many home cooks are put off by the myth that hollandaise sauce is difficult to make. The recipe in this section, made with the aid of a blender or food processor, is very simple and can be kept warm in an insulated coffee cup (the type that you can buy in any main street coffee store). It is so easy that you will find yourself wondering what all the fuss was about.

Equally simple and delicious is my recipe for Baked Eggs with Cream, Spinach, and Parmesan. Served in individual portions, the eggs are baked until the whites are just set, creating a gloriously golden sauce over the spinach. They take only minutes to prepare and, served with warm bread, make a satisfying brunch dish.

For a more substantial dish, try the Tortilla with Roasted Bell Peppers, and Spicy Chorizo. The tortilla can be enjoyed straight from the skillet or cut into wedges and served with a green salad for a more formal presentation.

Finally, for anyone who finds the prospect of soufflés daunting, my advice is simple—don't worry. The recipe for Cheese and Herb Soufflés is the twice-baked variety, which is both delicious and more robust. Follow the tips in the recipe for a guaranteed stress free result.

For best results when poaching eggs, break them into a cup first, then slide them into the hot water. Poach for a little longer than the suggested three minutes if you prefer firmer yolks.

Eggs Benedict with Quick Hollandaise Sauce

SERVES 4

Fill a wide skillet three-quarters full with water and bring to a boil over low heat. Reduce the heat to a simmer and add the vinegar. When the water is barely shimmering, carefully break the eggs into the skillet. Let stand for 1 minute, then, using a large spoon, gently loosen the eggs from the bottom of the skillet. Let cook for an additional 3 minutes, or until the white is cooked and the yolk is still soft, basting the top of the egg with the water from time to time.

Meanwhile, to make the hollandaise sauce, place the egg yolks in a blender or food processor. Melt the butter in a small pan until bubbling. With the motor running, gradually add the hot butter in a steady stream until the sauce is thick and creamy. Add the lemon juice, and a little warm water if the sauce is too thick, then season to taste with pepper. Remove from the blender or food processor and keep warm.

Split the muffins and toast them on both sides. To serve, top each muffin with a slice of ham, a poached egg, and a generous spoonful of hollandaise sauce.

INGREDIENTS
1 tbsp white wine vinegar
4 eggs
4 English muffins
4 slices good quality ham
QUICK HOLLANDAISE SAUCE
3 egg yolks
7 oz/200 g butter
1 tbsp lemon juice
pepper

CAUTION
Recipes using raw eggs should be avoided by infants, the elderly, pregnant women, convalescents, and anyone suffering from an illness.

As a variation, try substituting smoked trout and snipped chives or even fresh crabmeat—delicious!

Scrambled Eggs with Smoked Salmon

INGREDIENTS

8 eggs

⅓ cup light cream

2 tbsp chopped fresh dill, plus extra
    for garnishing

salt and pepper

3½ oz/100 g smoked salmon, cut into
    small pieces

2 tbsp butter

slices rustic bread, toasted

SERVES 4

Break the eggs into a large bowl and whisk together with the cream and dill. Season to taste with salt and pepper. Add the smoked salmon and mix to combine.

Melt the butter in a large nonstick skillet and pour in the egg and smoked salmon mixture. Using a wooden spatula, gently scrape the egg away from the sides of the skillet as it starts to set and swirl the skillet slightly to allow the uncooked egg to fill the surface.

When the eggs are almost cooked but still creamy, remove from the heat and spoon onto the prepared toast. Serve at once, garnished with a sprig of dill.

Manchego cheese is a firm Spanish cheese made from sheep's milk. Substitute a good quality Parmesan or romano if you have trouble finding it. Don't add oil when cooking the chorizo sausage as it already contains a high percentage of fat.

Tortilla with Roasted Bell Peppers & Spicy Chorizo

SERVES 6

Preheat the oven to 400°F/200°C. Place the red bell peppers on a lined baking sheet and roast for 15 minutes, or until the skins are black. Remove from the oven and cover with a dish towel until cool. When cool, peel away the skins and dice the flesh.

Meanwhile, cook the diced chorizo in a 12-inch/30-cm nonstick skillet until it is brown and the fat is rendered. Drain on paper towels. Wipe out the skillet, then heat the oil and cook the diced potatoes for 5 minutes, or until soft and lightly browned. Return the chorizo to the skillet with the potatoes and add the diced red bell peppers and torn basil leaves.

Mix the eggs and grated cheese together and season to taste with salt and pepper. Pour over the ingredients in the skillet, using a wooden spoon to distribute the ingredients evenly. Let cook for a few minutes over low heat until the egg has started to set. To finish the tortilla, place the skillet under a preheated hot broiler to brown lightly. Slide onto a serving plate and cut into wedges to serve.

INGREDIENTS

2 red bell peppers, halved and seeded
2 small chorizo sausages, diced
1 tbsp olive oil
2 potatoes, peeled and diced
handful of fresh basil leaves, torn into pieces
6 large eggs, lightly beaten
6 tbsp grated Manchego cheese
salt and pepper

Make the caramelized onions in advance and store in the refrigerator for up to a week. If the batter mixture for the fritters seems too thick, stir in a little extra milk.

Zucchini Fritters with Eggs & Caramelized Onions

INGREDIENTS
2 tbsp extra virgin olive oil
5 red onions, sliced
1 tbsp brown sugar
salt and pepper
scant 1½ cups self-rising flour
1 egg, lightly beaten, plus 4 eggs
    for poaching or frying
scant 1 cup milk
2 zucchini, grated
1 cup corn oil

SERVES 4

Heat the olive oil in a large heavy-bottom pan over medium heat, add the onions, and cook for 5 minutes, or until softened. Stir in the sugar and reduce the heat, cover, and cook for 30 minutes, or until the onions are deep brown in color, stirring occasionally. Season to taste with salt and pepper and let cool.

To make the fritters, place the flour in a large bowl and make a well in the center. Whisk the beaten egg and milk together and incorporate into the flour, using a wooden spoon to make a batter. Season to taste with salt and pepper and stir in the grated zucchini.

Heat the corn oil in a wide deep-sided pan and drop in tablespoons of the batter. Cook until golden brown on both sides, turning once. Drain on paper towels and keep warm.

Poach or fry the eggs, as you prefer. To serve, place 2 fritters on each individual plate, place an egg on top, and spoon over some of the caramelized onions. Serve at once.

The Tomato Chili Jelly can be made up to three months in advance and stored in the cupboard. Refrigerate once the jelly has been opened. Cheddar cheese makes a nice alternative to fontina.

Sandwiches with Tomato Chili Jelly

SERVES 2

To make the tomato chili jelly, heat the oil in a medium pan over low heat and cook the diced onion for 5 minutes, or until soft but not brown. Add the diced red bell pepper and red pepper flakes and cook for an additional 2 minutes, then add the tomatoes, vinegar, and sugar. Bring to a boil, then reduce the heat and let simmer for 45 minutes, stirring occasionally, until the mixture thickens to a jelly consistency.

Divide the cheese between 2 slices of bread. Spread each with a tablespoon of the tomato chili jelly and cover with another slice of bread. Beat the eggs and salt and pepper to taste in a wide dish. Dip one side of each sandwich into the egg mixture and let stand for 1 minute. Repeat with the other side.

Heat the butter in a small nonstick skillet over low heat and add one sandwich at a time. Cook for 2 minutes, or until golden brown and the cheese is starting to melt, then turn and cook for an additional 2 minutes. Repeat with the remaining sandwich.

Serve with a handful of fresh arugula leaves and some more tomato chili jelly on the side.

INGREDIENTS

4 slices fontina cheese
4 slices bread
3 eggs
salt and pepper
2 tbsp butter
arugula leaves, to serve
TOMATO CHILI JELLY
1 tbsp corn oil
1 onion, diced
1 red bell pepper, seeded and diced
1 tbsp dried red pepper flakes
2 large tomatoes, chopped
generous 1 cup cider vinegar
generous ½ cup brown sugar

As a variation, add some diced ham or smoked salmon to the cooked spinach. The quantity of baby spinach used in this recipe may seem a lot but it shrinks substantially as it cooks.

Baked Eggs with Cream, Spinach & Parmesan

INGREDIENTS
2 tbsp butter, plus extra for greasing
scant 3 cups baby spinach
½ tsp freshly grated nutmeg
4 small eggs
¼ cup light cream
2 tbsp freshly grated Parmesan cheese
salt and pepper

SERVES 2
Preheat the oven to 325°F/160°C. Lightly grease 2 individual ceramic gratin dishes or similar.

Melt the butter in a large skillet over low heat and add the spinach. Cook for 1 minute, stirring with a wooden spoon until the spinach starts to wilt. Season with a little nutmeg, then divide between the prepared dishes.

Gently break 2 eggs into each dish. Pour the cream over them, and sprinkle with grated Parmesan, then season to taste with salt and pepper. Bake for 10 minutes, or until the whites of the eggs have set but the yolks remain runny. Serve at once.

Do not be tempted to overfill the soufflé dishes, since the mixture may rise and fall over the sides. For best results, use only very fresh eggs. The cooked soufflés without the topping will keep for up to 24 hours in the refrigerator.

Cheese & Herb Soufflés with Sautéed Mushrooms

MAKES 6 SOUFFLÉS

Preheat the oven to 350°F/180°C. Brush 6 x 3½-inch/9-cm soufflé dishes well with melted butter and set aside. Melt the butter in a medium pan, add the flour, and cook for 30 seconds, stirring constantly. Whisk in the milk and continue whisking over low heat until the mixture thickens. Cook for an additional 30 seconds. Remove from the heat and beat in the ricotta. Add the egg yolks and herbs and season well with salt and pepper.

Beat the egg whites in a clean bowl until they form stiff peaks and gently fold them through the ricotta mixture. Spoon into the prepared dishes, filling them just to the top. Place in a baking dish and pour in enough boiling water to come halfway up the sides of the dishes. Bake for 15–20 minutes, or until the soufflés are well risen and browned. Remove from the oven, let cool for 10 minutes, then gently ease out of their molds. Place in a lightly greased ovenproof dish and cover with plastic wrap.

Increase the oven temperature to 400°F/200°C. Remove the plastic wrap and pour the cream evenly over the soufflés, sprinkle with Parmesan, and return to the oven for an additional 15 minutes. Serve at once with sautéed mushrooms.

INGREDIENTS

2 oz/55 g butter, plus extra, melted, for greasing
⅓ cup all-purpose flour
⅔ cup milk
generous 1 cup ricotta cheese
4 egg yolks
2 tbsp finely chopped fresh parsley
2 tbsp finely chopped fresh thyme
1 tbsp finely chopped fresh rosemary
salt and pepper
6 egg whites
scant 1 cup light cream
6 tbsp grated Parmesan cheese
sautéed white mushrooms, to serve

This torte is delicious served hot or warm. It can be made a few hours in advance and reheated in a cool oven just before serving.

Omelet Torte with Indian Spices

INGREDIENTS

2 tbsp vegetable oil

1 small red onion, diced

1 tbsp fennel seeds

1 tsp dried red pepper flakes

9 oz/250 g canned chickpeas, drained and rinsed

1 cup frozen peas, thawed

1 tomato, diced

8 eggs

3 tbsp chopped fresh cilantro

salt and pepper

TO SERVE

4 tbsp tomato chutney

4 tbsp plain yogurt

SERVES 4

Preheat the broiler to hot. Heat the oil in a 12-inch/30-cm nonstick skillet over low heat and cook the onion for a few minutes, or until soft but not brown. Add the fennel seeds and red pepper flakes and cook for an additional 1 minute, then stir in the chickpeas, peas, and diced tomato.

Break the eggs into a bowl and beat lightly with a fork. Mix in the cilantro and season to taste with salt and pepper. Pour the egg mixture over the ingredients in the skillet and cook until just starting to set. Place under the broiler until the egg has fully set and the torte is lightly brown. Serve, cut into wedges, with tomato chutney and yogurt on the side.

Resist the temptation to cook the eggs completely. The best scrambled eggs should still look just a little undercooked—they will carry on cooking in their own heat once you have served them.

Chive Scrambled Eggs with Brioche

SERVES 2

Break the eggs into a medium bowl and whisk gently with the cream. Season to taste with salt and pepper and add the snipped chives.

Melt the butter in a sauté pan and pour in the egg mixture. Let set slightly, then move the mixture toward the center of the pan using a wooden spoon as the eggs start to cook. Continue in this way until the eggs are cooked but still creamy.

Place the toasted brioche slices in the center of 2 plates and spoon over the scrambled eggs. Serve at once, garnished with whole chives.

INGREDIENTS

4 eggs
generous ⅓ cup light cream
salt and pepper
2 tbsp snipped fresh chives, plus
    4 whole fresh chives to garnish
2 tbsp butter
4 slices brioche loaf, lightly toasted

Vegetable bouillon granules make an excellent substitute for fresh stock if you don't have it to hand. Simply measure out 2½ cups of hot water and stir in 2 tablespoons of the bouillon granules.

Smoked Trout Kedgeree

INGREDIENTS

2 oz/55 g butter
1 tbsp corn oil
1 onion, diced
1 tbsp garam masala
1 tsp ground turmeric
4 cardamom pods, lightly crushed
1 cinnamon stick
generous 1¼ cups long-grain rice
2½ cups water
2 tbsp vegetable bouillon granules
9 oz/250 g smoked trout fillets
3 hard-cooked eggs, shelled
1 tbsp chopped fresh parsley
1 tbsp snipped fresh chives
1 tbsp chopped fresh dill

SERVES 4–6

Melt the butter with the oil in a 12-inch/30-cm nonstick skillet and cook the onion for 5 minutes over low heat, or until soft but not brown. Add the garam masala, turmeric, cardamom pods, and cinnamon stick and cook for an additional 1 minute, then add the rice, stirring to coat well.

Pour over the water and bouillon granules. Bring to a boil, then reduce the heat and cook over very low heat for 20 minutes, stirring from time to time, until the rice is tender, adding more water if necessary.

Flake the smoked trout into bite-size pieces and quarter the hard-cooked eggs. Reserve a small amount of the trout for garnish. Stir the remainder through the rice mixture gently, together with the chopped herbs, reserving a little for the garnish. Transfer the kedgeree to a serving bowl and sprinkle with the reserved smoked trout and herbs. Serve at once.

cheese a

cheese and greens

Brunch is eaten at that gloriously lazy time somewhere between late morning and early afternoon, so it lends itself to many different options. It is one of the most exciting meals for any enthusiastic cook since there are no hard and fast rules.

With that in mind, this chapter encourages a break from some of the more traditional brunch dishes. But remember, while you can serve anything that inspires you, it is important to use only the best quality ingredients that are in season. The recipe for Fresh Asparagus Topped with Bread Crumbs and Chopped Eggs, with its crunchy topping, for example, relies heavily on the quality of the asparagus used. If you can't find good quality asparagus, save the recipe for another day.

Interesting salads make a wonderful brunch course, particularly if you are preparing a selection of dishes for friends. The recipe for Roasted Figs with Bayonne Ham, Baby Spinach, and Balsamic Glaze highlights the versatility of balsamic vinegar. It is a simple yet flavorful condiment that will find a multitude of uses in your kitchen.

The Mini Bacon and Egg Pastries with Cheddar are perfect if you are catering for a crowd. The base of the pastries has a surprise tang to it, thanks to a dash of whole-grain mustard, but feel free to experiment with your own combinations. I have used diced olives, chopped herbs, and even a dash of harissa (a spicy chili paste) in the past with great success. The other bonus of these little pastries is that they make great picnic food.

A little chili in this recipe is delicious, but be sure to choose a mild chili so that the result is not too overpowering.

Mushrooms with Rosemary, Chili, Sour Cream & Arugula

SERVES 2

Wipe the mushrooms with a damp cloth and slice thinly.

Heat the butter and vegetable oil in a wide sauté pan and add the mushrooms, stirring until well coated. Season lightly with salt and pepper and add the chopped chili. Cover and cook for 1–2 minutes, or until the mushrooms have softened, then stir in the sour cream. Sprinkle over the chopped parsley and rosemary.

Serve with slices of toasted ciabatta, drizzled lightly with olive oil, topped with a few arugula leaves.

INGREDIENTS

10½ oz/300 g white mushrooms
1 tbsp butter
1 tbsp vegetable oil
salt and pepper
1 small fresh red chili, seeded and finely chopped
1 tbsp sour cream
2 tbsp chopped fresh parsley
1 tbsp chopped fresh rosemary
TO SERVE
slices ciabatta bread, toasted
extra virgin olive oil
handful of arugula leaves

Take care not to force the dough circles into the muffin pans by stretching them as this will lead to the dough shrinking while it is in the oven. Gently ease the dough into the pan so that it fits into the edges before filling the pastries.

Mini Bacon & Egg Pastries with Cheddar

INGREDIENTS
butter, for greasing

1 lb 2 oz/500 g prepared basic pie dough

all-purpose flour, for rolling

2 tbsp whole-grain mustard

12 lean bacon slices, diced, cooked, and drained well

12 small eggs

pepper

generous 1 cup grated Cheddar cheese

2 tbsp chopped fresh parsley

MAKES 12 PASTRIES

Preheat the oven to 350°F/180°C. Lightly grease a deep 12-cup muffin pan.

Roll the dough out to a ¼-inch/5-mm thickness on a lightly floured counter and cut out 12 circles approximately 5 inches/13 cm in diameter. Use to line the cups of the muffin pan, gently pleating the sides of the dough as you ease it into the molds. Place ½ teaspoon of the mustard into the base of each pastry shell and top with a little of the bacon.

Break an egg into a cup, spoon the yolk into the pastry shell, then add enough of the white to fill the pastry shell about two-thirds full. Do not overfill. Season to taste with pepper and sprinkle the grated cheese evenly over the tops of the pastries. Bake for 20–25 minutes, or until the egg is set and the cheese is golden brown. Serve warm, sprinkled with chopped parsley.

Bayonne ham is a delicious cured ham from France.
Substitute prosciutto if this is unavailable.

Roasted Figs with Bayonne Ham, Baby Spinach & Balsamic Glaze

SERVES 4

Preheat the oven to 325°F/160°C. Wipe over the figs, brush them with a little oil, and place on a lightly oiled baking sheet. Bake for 10–12 minutes, or until the figs are soft but still retain their shape. Remove from the oven and let cool. When cool, cut into quarters.

To make the glaze, place the balsamic vinegar, honey, and butter in a small pan and bring to a boil. Reduce the heat and let simmer for 5 minutes. Season to taste with salt and pepper and let cool.

When you are ready to serve, divide the spinach evenly between 4 plates. Arrange the Bayonne ham on top and follow with the quartered roasted figs. Drizzle over a little of the balsamic glaze and serve with crusty bread.

INGREDIENTS

4 fresh figs
1 tbsp olive oil, plus extra
 for oiling
scant 3 cups baby spinach
8 slices Bayonne ham
crusty bread, to serve
BALSAMIC GLAZE
⅓ cup good quality
 balsamic vinegar
2 tbsp honey
2 tbsp butter
salt and pepper

This recipe makes more spice mixture than you will need but it is difficult to make less. Store the leftover mixture in an airtight container for up to two months. Try it on broiled chicken or steak for a quick lunch or dinner dish.

Seared Salmon with Quick Hollandaise Sauce & Baby Spinach

INGREDIENTS

1 tbsp each dried thyme, dried rosemary, dried oregano, and mild paprika

1 tsp garlic powder

2 tsp cumin seeds

1 tbsp sea salt

4 salmon fillets, skin removed

1 tbsp vegetable oil

scant 3½ cups baby spinach

QUICK HOLLANDAISE SAUCE

3 egg yolks

7 oz/200 g butter

1 tbsp lemon juice

pepper

CAUTION
Recipes using raw eggs should be avoided by infants, the elderly, pregnant women, convalescents, and anyone suffering from an illness.

SERVES 4

Combine the dried herbs, paprika, garlic powder, cumin seeds, and sea salt in a small grinder and process until smooth. Alternatively, grind by hand using a pestle in a mortar. Rub 1 tablespoon of the mixture into the top of each of the salmon fillets.

Heat the oil in a large skillet and cook the salmon, spice-side down, for 2–3 minutes, or until golden brown. Turn over and continue cooking until the salmon is cooked to your liking. Do not overcook or the salmon will be dry.

To make the hollandaise sauce, place the egg yolks in a blender or food processor. Melt the butter in a small pan until bubbling. With the motor running, gradually add the hot butter in a steady stream until the sauce is thick and creamy. Add the lemon juice, and a little warm water if the sauce is too thick, then season to taste with pepper. Remove from the blender or food processor and keep warm.

Divide the baby spinach equally between 4 plates, place the cooked salmon on top, and spoon over the sauce. Serve at once.

Phyllo pastry dries out very quickly, so be sure to keep unused portions covered with a damp cloth as you work.

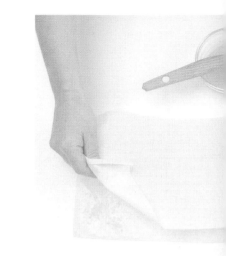

Smoked Salmon, Feta & Dill Phyllo Packages

MAKES 6 PACKAGES

Preheat the oven to 350°F/180°C. Lightly grease a baking sheet. In a large bowl, combine the feta, ricotta, smoked salmon, dill, and chives. Season to taste with pepper.

Lay out a sheet of pastry on your counter and brush well with melted butter. Sprinkle over 2 teaspoons of the bread crumbs and cover with a second sheet of pastry. Brush with butter and spread a large tablespoon of the salmon mixture on one end of the pastry. Roll the pastry up, folding in the sides, to enclose the salmon completely and create a neat package. Place on the prepared baking sheet, brush the top of the package with butter and sprinkle over 1 teaspoon of the fennel seeds. Repeat with the remaining ingredients to make 6 packages.

Bake the packages for 25–30 minutes, or until the pastry is golden brown. Serve the packages warm.

INGREDIENTS

5½ oz/150 g feta cheese, crumbled
generous 1 cup ricotta cheese
5½ oz/150 g smoked salmon, diced
2 tbsp chopped fresh dill
2 tbsp snipped fresh chives
salt and pepper
12 sheets phyllo pastry
3½ oz/100 g butter, melted, plus extra
  for greasing
4 tbsp dried bread crumbs
6 tsp fennel seeds

Harissa is a spicy Middle Eastern paste that is available in most large supermarkets. Chorizo can be purchased in a mild or spicy form. Choose whichever type you prefer.

Lima Bean, Red Onion, Herb Salad & Spicy Sausage

INGREDIENTS

1 tbsp corn oil

1 small red onion, finely sliced

9 oz/250 g canned lima beans, drained and rinsed

1 tsp balsamic vinegar

2 chorizo sausages, cut into diagonal slices

1 small tomato, diced

2 tbsp harissa paste

3 oz/85 g mixed herb salad

SERVES 2

Heat the oil in a medium nonstick skillet and cook the onion until softened but not brown. Add the lima beans and cook for an additional 1 minute, then add the balsamic vinegar, stirring well. Keep warm.

In another skillet, cook the chorizo slices until lightly brown and let drain on paper towels.

Mix the diced tomato and harissa paste together. Divide the herb salad between 2 plates, spoon over the lima bean mixture, and place the warm chorizo on top. Place a spoonful of the tomato and harissa mixture on top and serve at once.

Use the grater blade on your food processor to make the job of grating the sweet potato really easy. Serve with slices of smoked salmon or crispy bacon for an interesting variation.

Sweet Potato, Mint & Feta Rösti

SERVES 4

Preheat the oven to 325°F/160°C. Cover a baking sheet with parchment paper. Mix the grated sweet potato with the egg, flour, melted butter, feta, and mint until well combined. Season to taste with salt and pepper.

Heat the oil in a large nonstick skillet over medium heat. Spoon large tablespoons of the mixture into patties, flattening slightly, and cook on both sides in batches until golden.

Slide the rösti on to the prepared baking sheet and bake for 15 minutes, or until crisp. Place 2 rösti on each plate, top with a tablespoon of sour cream, and garnish with a little chopped parsley. Serve at once.

INGREDIENTS

1 lb 5 oz/600 g sweet potatoes, peeled and grated

1 egg, lightly beaten

⅓ cup all-purpose flour

2½ oz/70 g butter, melted

3½ oz/100 g feta cheese, crumbled

3 tbsp chopped fresh mint

salt and pepper

1 tbsp vegetable oil

4 tbsp sour cream

2 tbsp chopped fresh parsley, to garnish

The simplest way to make fresh bread crumbs is to cut the crusts off a stale loaf of bread, break the bread into large pieces and process briefly in a food processor. You can store the bread crumbs in plastic bags in the freezer for up to three months.

Asparagus Topped with Bread Crumbs & Chopped Eggs

INGREDIENTS
3½ oz/100 g butter

1¾ cups fresh white bread crumbs

2 hard-cooked eggs, shelled and chopped

2 tbsp chopped fresh parsley

salt and pepper

2 lb 4 oz/1 kg fresh asparagus, trimmed

juice of 1 lemon

SERVES 4

Melt the butter in a large skillet. Set aside half of the melted butter for pouring over the finished dish. Add the bread crumbs to the melted butter in the skillet, stirring constantly until they are golden brown. Turn onto a baking sheet to cool and crisp, then combine with the chopped hard-cooked egg and parsley. Season to taste with salt and pepper.

Bring a large pan of salted water to a boil and cook the asparagus until just tender. Drain and place on a large serving platter. Mix the remaining butter with the lemon juice and pour over the asparagus. Sprinkle the bread crumbs over the top and serve hot or warm.

Look for a really good quality feta cheese that isn't too salty for this recipe. As an alternative, try this recipe with slices of fresh buffalo mozzarella.

Broiled Feta Cheese with Chili on Ciabatta Toast

SERVES 2

Preheat the broiler to hot. Place the toasted ciabatta slices on a baking sheet and cover each with a generous slice of feta cheese. Mix the oil, red pepper flakes, and oregano together and drizzle evenly over the cheese.

Cook under the preheated broiler for 2–3 minutes, or until the cheese starts to melt, and place on serving plates. Drizzle over a little extra oil and serve with arugula leaves.

INGREDIENTS

4 slices ciabatta bread, lightly toasted
7 oz/200 g feta cheese
2 tbsp olive oil, plus extra for drizzling
1 tsp dried red pepper flakes
1 tsp dried oregano
scant 2 cups arugula leaves, to serve

Mushrooms absorb water, so never soak them to clean them. The best way to clean them is simply to wipe them over with a damp cloth. For Parmesan shavings, run a vegetable peeler down the side of the cheese.

Stuffed Portobello Mushrooms with Shaved Parmesan

INGREDIENTS

12 large portobello mushrooms, wiped over and stems removed

2 tbsp corn oil, plus extra for oiling

1 fennel bulb, stalks removed, finely chopped

scant ½ cup sun-dried tomatoes, finely chopped

2 garlic cloves, crushed

generous 1 cup grated fontina cheese

scant ½ cup freshly grated Parmesan cheese

3 tbsp chopped fresh basil

salt and pepper

1 tbsp olive oil

TO SERVE

fresh Parmesan cheese shavings

1 tbsp chopped fresh parsley

SERVES 4

Preheat the oven to 350°F/180°C. Lightly oil a large ovenproof dish. Place 8 of the mushrooms, cup-side up, in the dish and chop the remaining 4 mushrooms finely.

Heat the corn oil in a nonstick skillet, add the chopped mushrooms, fennel, sun-dried tomatoes, and garlic and cook over low heat until the vegetables are soft but not browned. Remove from the heat and let cool.

When cool, add the cheeses, basil, and salt and pepper to taste. Mix well. Brush the mushrooms lightly with the olive oil and fill each cavity with a spoonful of the vegetable filling. Bake for 20–25 minutes, or until the mushrooms are tender and the filling is heated through.

Top with Parmesan shavings and parsley and serve at once, allowing 2 mushrooms for each person.

toasts a

toasts and tarts

This chapter has a little something for everyone, from a simple method for honey-glazed bacon to a twist on the conventional French favorite, the Croque Monsieur. Perfect for a late-morning brunch, these recipes will please the heartiest of appetites.

Nothing is more satisfying to make than homemade bread and my recipe for Focaccia with Roasted Cherry Tomatoes, Basil, and Crispy Pancetta is simple to make and tastes wonderful. The secret to the quality of this bread lies in the kneading, a process which is very therapeutic. For those cooks for whom kneading has the opposite effect, invest in a freestanding electric mixer with a dough attachment, which will give you an equally enjoyable result. A lot less time-consuming is my recipe for Tuscan Beans on Ciabatta Toast with Fresh Herbs. Deliciously simple, these are a great version of homemade baked beans, which make a nice change from the canned variety and only take moments to prepare.

The recipe for Smoked Salmon, Red Onion, and Goat Cheese Tarts is very simple to make using ready-made puff pastry. Making your own pastry is easy, but if time is of the essence, buy the best quality pastry that you can find. Some cake stores still make their own pastry and may be willing to sell it to you. If so, buy a manageable quantity and store it in your freezer until required.

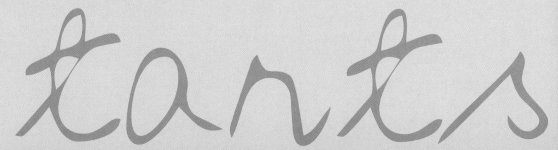

Glazing the bacon in this way gives it a lovely sweet flavor, but don't leave it over the heat for too long as the honey tends to burn very quickly. Use maple syrup in the same way for a slightly different flavor.

Toasted English Muffins with Honey-Glazed Bacon & Eggs

SERVES 2

Heat a nonstick skillet over medium heat. Lay the bacon slices in the skillet and cook until lightly browned, then turn and cook the other side.

Warm the honey slightly and brush each bacon slice lightly with it. Cook the bacon for an additional 1 minute or so until it takes on a slight glaze. Remove from the skillet and keep warm.

Mix the corn, diced tomatoes, and chopped parsley together and season to taste with salt and pepper. Fry, poach, or scramble the eggs, as you prefer.

Serve the honey-glazed bacon and eggs on buttered toasted English muffins, topped with a spoonful of the corn and tomato mixture.

INGREDIENTS

6 rindless unsmoked bacon slices

1 tbsp honey

3 oz/85 g canned corn kernels, drained

2 small tomatoes, diced

1 tbsp chopped fresh parsley

salt and pepper

4 eggs

2 English muffins, split, toasted, and buttered

For the best results, use very cold ingredients. The amount of water required will vary depending on the weather conditions, so just use enough to bring the ingredients together to form a dough.

Ricotta & Tomato Freeform Tart

INGREDIENTS

generous 1½ cups all-purpose flour, plus extra for rolling

6 oz/175 g cold butter, cut into small pieces, plus extra for greasing

1 tsp dried thyme

salt and pepper

FILLING

generous 1 cup ricotta cheese

2 eggs, lightly beaten

4 tbsp heavy cream

2 tbsp freshly grated Parmesan cheese

1 tsp dried thyme

salt and pepper

2 ripe tomatoes, sliced

1 tbsp milk, for glazing

SERVES 4–6

Preheat the oven to 350°F/180°C. Lightly grease a 11½-inch/29-cm pie pan. Place the flour and butter in the bowl of a food processor and pulse until the mixture resembles bread crumbs. Add the thyme and salt and pepper to taste. With the motor running, pour in just enough cold water to make a firm dough.

Turn the dough out onto a lightly floured counter and bring it together to form a ball. Roll the dough into a circle large enough to fit the pie pan. Line the pan with the dough, trimming the dough edge evenly with the edge of the pan.

To make the filling, mix the ricotta, eggs, cream, Parmesan, and thyme together in a bowl and season to taste with salt and pepper. Gently pour the mixture into the pastry shell and top with the tomato slices. Fold the dough gently over the filling to form a rim and brush with milk. Bake for 40–45 minutes, or until the filling is set and the pastry is golden brown. Serve warm or cold.

This leek and Gruyère cheese mixture is a perfect topping for bagels, but also tastes delicious served on slices of sourdough toast, for a change.

Bagels with Leeks & Cheese

SERVES 2

Trim the leeks, discarding the green ends, and split down the center, leaving the root intact. Wash well to remove any grit and slice finely, discarding the root.

Melt the butter over low heat in a large sauté pan and add the leeks. Cook, stirring constantly, for 5 minutes, or until the leeks are soft and slightly browned. Let cool.

Preheat the broiler. Mix the cooled leeks, grated cheese, scallions, parsley, and salt and pepper to taste together. Split the bagels and toast lightly on the bottom. Spread the cheese mixture over the top of each bagel and place under the preheated broiler until bubbling and golden brown. Serve at once.

INGREDIENTS

2 leeks
2 tbsp butter
generous 1 cup grated Gruyère cheese
2 scallions, finely chopped
salt and pepper
1 tbsp chopped fresh parsley
2 fresh bagels

Vary this recipe by experimenting with different kinds of bread, such as rye or sourdough. Although ham is the traditional filling for this classic French sandwich, slices of turkey or roast chicken make delicious alternatives.

Croque Monsieur

INGREDIENTS
1 tbsp butter
4 slices bread
4 thin slices good quality ham
4 tbsp grated mozzarella cheese
2 tbsp plain yogurt
salt and pepper
1 tbsp chopped fresh parsley

SERVES 2

Butter the bread slices and sandwich them, buttered-sides together. Place the ham on top of the sandwiches and sprinkle a little of the grated cheese over the top.

Heat a nonstick skillet large enough to take 2 sandwiches. Place the top slices of bread (with the ham and cheese on top), buttered-side down, into the skillet. Top with the remaining slices of bread, buttered-side up. Cook until the base of each sandwich is golden brown.

Preheat the broiler to hot. Mix the remaining cheese, yogurt, and salt and pepper to taste together. Remove the skillet from the heat and spread an equal quantity of the yogurt mixture on top of each sandwich. Place under the preheated broiler and cook until lightly browned. Sprinkle with the chopped parsley and serve.

Weighting the dough when baking an empty pastry shell prevents it rising during baking, leaving plenty of room for the filling. If you don't have dried beans, use rice or dried lentils for a similar result.

Provençal Tart

SERVES 6

Preheat the oven to 350°F/180°C. Place the flour and butter in the bowl of a food processor and pulse until the mixture resembles bread crumbs. Add the Parmesan, salt and pepper to taste, and the egg yolk and pulse again. With the motor running, gradually add just enough cold water until the mixture forms a dough.

Turn out onto a lightly floured counter and gently press the dough together. Roll out to about ¼ inch/5 mm thick and use to line a 9½-inch/24-cm shallow loose-bottom tart ring. Prick the dough with a fork, then line with parchment paper and fill with dried beans. Bake for 20 minutes, then remove the beans and paper and bake for an additional 5–10 minutes, or until golden brown. Remove from the oven and let cool.

Cover a baking sheet with parchment paper. Lay out the zucchini slices in a single layer. Sprinkle the oil over the top and season to taste with salt and pepper. Bake for 20 minutes, or until lightly browned. Transfer to the pastry shell and top with the tomato slices. Sprinkle the basil and grated cheeses over the mixture and bake for 15 minutes, or until the cheese has melted. Serve warm, cut into wedges.

INGREDIENTS

scant 1½ cups all-purpose flour, plus extra
    for rolling
4½ oz/125 g butter, cut into small pieces
4 tbsp freshly grated Parmesan cheese
salt and pepper
1 egg yolk
FILLING
2 zucchini, sliced
1 tbsp olive oil
salt and pepper
3 large tomatoes, sliced
4 tbsp fresh basil leaves, torn
2 oz/55 g mozzarella cheese, grated
2 oz/55 g Cheddar cheese, grated

Prepare the topping ingredients up to one hour in advance, adding the avocado and balsamic vinegar just before serving. Buffalo mozzarella is widely available from good delicatessens and large supermarkets.

Brunch Bruschetta

INGREDIENTS
1 large ripe tomato, diced

2 scallions, finely sliced

1 small fresh buffalo mozzarella cheese, diced

½ ripe avocado, diced

½ tbsp balsamic vinegar

2 tbsp extra virgin olive oil

salt and pepper

4 slices ciabatta bread, toasted, to serve

2 tbsp shredded fresh basil leaves, to garnish

SERVES 2

Mix the tomato, scallions, cheese, avocado, balsamic vinegar, and half of the oil together in a medium bowl. Season to taste with salt and pepper.

Drizzle the remaining oil over the ciabatta toast and top with the tomato mixture. Garnish with basil and serve at once.

Be sure to roll the final bread dough out fairly thinly as it rises quite a bit in the final stage. Take care not to bake the tomatoes for too long, otherwise they will lose their shape.

Focaccia with Roasted Cherry Tomatoes, Basil & Crispy Pancetta

SERVES 4–6

Place the flour, dried basil, sugar, yeast, and salt in a bowl. Combine the water and oil and mix with the dry ingredients to form a soft dough, adding more water if the dough appears too dry. Turn out onto a lightly floured counter and knead for 10 minutes, or until the dough bounces back when pressed lightly with your finger. Place the dough in a lightly oiled bowl and cover with plastic wrap. Leave in a warm place for 1 hour, or until doubled in size.

Meanwhile, preheat the oven to 275°F/140°C. Place the tomatoes on a baking sheet covered with parchment paper, sprinkle with oil, and season to taste with salt and pepper. Bake for 30 minutes, or until the tomatoes are soft.

Increase the oven temperature to 425°F/220°C. Remove the dough from the bowl and knead again briefly. Shape into a rectangle and place on a lightly oiled baking sheet, turning the dough over to oil both sides. Make rough indentations in the dough using your fingers. Top with the tomatoes and pancetta. Sprinkle with salt and pepper. Leave in a warm place for 10 minutes for the dough to rise again. Bake for 15–20 minutes, or until golden brown and cooked through. Drizzle with oil and top with fresh basil. Serve warm.

INGREDIENTS

1 lb 2 oz/500 g white bread flour, plus extra for kneading and rolling

1 tbsp dried basil

½ tsp sugar

2 tsp active dry yeast

2 tsp salt

generous 1¼ cups water, lukewarm

2 tbsp olive oil, plus extra for oiling

TOPPING

14 oz/400 g cherry tomatoes

1 tbsp olive oil, plus extra for oiling and drizzling

salt and pepper

7 oz/200 g thick pancetta, diced

4 tbsp chopped fresh basil

Look for puff pastry made with butter for the very best results. There are many different types of goat cheese available—a mild, creamy variety is perfect for this recipe. Substitute with Camembert or Brie, cut into pieces, if you prefer.

Smoked Salmon, Red Onion & Goat Cheese Tarts

INGREDIENTS
9 oz/250 g good quality puff pastry
all-purpose flour, for rolling
1 egg, lightly beaten with 1 tbsp milk
1 small red onion, sliced
3½ oz/100 g goat cheese, crumbled
4 slices smoked salmon
pepper

SERVES 4
Preheat the oven to 400°F/200°C. Roll the puff pastry out to ¼ inch/5 mm thick on a lightly floured counter and cut into 4 even-size squares. Place on an ungreased baking sheet and brush each square lightly with the egg mixture. Divide the sliced onion evenly between the tarts and top with goat cheese.

Bake for 20–25 minutes, or until the pastry has risen and is golden brown. Let cool slightly, then top with the slices of smoked salmon and season to taste with pepper. Serve at once.

This recipe also works well with cannellini beans. This dish can be made in advance and reheated as required.

Tuscan Beans on Ciabatta Toast with Fresh Herbs

SERVES 2

Heat the oil in a medium sauté pan and cook the onion over low heat until soft. Add the garlic and cook for an additional 1 minute, then add the lima beans, water, and tomato paste. Bring to a boil, stirring occasionally, and cook for 2 minutes.

Add the balsamic vinegar, parsley, and basil and stir to combine. Season to taste with salt and pepper and serve over slices of toasted ciabatta.

INGREDIENTS

1 tbsp olive oil

1 small onion, finely diced

1 garlic clove, crushed

9 oz/250 g canned lima beans, drained and rinsed

⅓ cup water

1 tbsp tomato paste

1 tsp balsamic vinegar

1 tbsp chopped fresh parsley

1 tbsp torn fresh basil

salt and pepper

slices ciabatta bread, toasted, to serve

Prepare the sausages up to 24 hours in advance and refrigerate them until required. Bake for 15 minutes before serving. Add fried, poached, or scrambled eggs for a real brunch feast!

Sausages with Mushrooms, Bacon, Tomatoes & Cooked Bread

INGREDIENTS
4 good quality herbed sausages
4 tbsp grated Cheddar cheese
4 unsmoked lean bacon slices
2 tomatoes, halved horizontally
salt and pepper
1 tbsp butter
1 tbsp olive oil
4½ oz/125 g white mushrooms, sliced
4 slices bread, crusts removed and
    buttered on both sides
2 tbsp chopped fresh parsley

SERVES 2

Preheat the oven to 350°F/180°C. Prick the sausages lightly, place in a roasting pan and roast for 10 minutes, or until just cooked. Remove and let cool. Make a slit in the sausages with a sharp knife and stuff each sausage with 1 tablespoon of the grated cheese. Wrap a bacon slice around each sausage, tucking in the ends to secure. Return to the oven for an additional 20 minutes, or until the bacon is cooked and the sausages are golden brown.

Meanwhile, place the tomatoes, cut-side up, on a baking sheet and season to taste with salt and pepper. Roast for 15–20 minutes. Melt the butter with the oil in a medium skillet over low heat, then add the mushrooms, stirring well to coat. Cover and cook for 5 minutes, or until the mushrooms are soft. Keep warm.

Heat a nonstick skillet over medium heat and cook the buttered bread in batches until golden brown on both sides. Keep warm.

To serve, divide the cooked bread between 2 plates and top with the mushrooms. Add the sausages and tomatoes and sprinkle with parsley.

index